THE

GIRL

GOD

WANTS

OTHER BOOKS
by
Daniella Whyte

- *THE THANKSGIVING THAT ALMOST WASN'T*
  (co-authored)

- *LETTERS TO YOUNG BLACK WOMEN*
  (co-authored)

THE GIRL GOD WANTS

Sister-to-sister talk on loving God, living
a great life, and enjoying it

by

DANIELLA WHYTE

THE GIRL GOD WANTS

Cover Design by Jack Kotowicz
Velocity Design Group

© Copyright 2007

TORCH LEGACY PUBLICATIONS, DALLAS, TEXAS;
ATLANTA, GEORGIA; BROOKLYN, NEW YORK

First Printing, 2007

The Bible quotations in this volume are from the King James Version of the Bible.

The name TORCH LEGACY PUBLICATIONS and its logo are registered as a trademark in the U.S. patent office.

ISBN: 0-9785333-4-8

Printed in the U.S.A.

This book is dedicated to:

My Papa and Mother:

Rev. & Mrs. Daniel Whyte III

My Sisters:

Danita, Danae', Daniqua, Danyelle Elizabeth, and Danielle

My Brothers:

Daniel IV, Danyel Ezekiel, and Duran

My Niece:

Kywaizia

My Grandmothers:

Shirley L. White & Hermoth K. Dixon

My Aunts:

Sheila Martin, Diane Dixon,
Temolynn Wintons and Stephanie White

My Female Cousins:

Chinara, Dinari, Milan White and Raevyn White-Jefferson.

And to

All young women around the world
who desire to be "the Girl God wants."

THE GIRL GOD WANTS
CONTENTS

The High Value of Education and Wisdom

It's All About Purpose and Passion

Purity Is Your Power

Walking on a Higher Plane

Inspired Living

INSPIRATIONS

ACKNOWLEDGEMENTS

Above all, I thank my Lord and Saviour Jesus Christ, by whom I live, move, and have my being, for giving me the opportunity to write this book, and for giving me the time to get it completed amidst other important work.

A very special thank you goes to my father, Daniel Whyte III, for encouraging me, for teaching me life's important lessons, and for passing on to me a great sense of humor; my mother, Meriqua Whyte, for helping to proofread and edit this book; my brother, Daniel IV, for being a good brother and friend and for helping in the proofreading process; and my youngest sisters and brother: Danita, Danae', Daniqua, Danyelle Elizabeth and Danyel Ezekiel for their love and support, and who always like to have a good time.

I would also like to thank Dianne Haskett and Jack Kotowicz for the wonderful job they did on the cover.

And to all young women who inspired me to write this book.

I pray this book will be a blessing and an encouragement to all who read it.

 # INTRODUCTION

In the short life that God has blessed me with, I acknowledge that I have not lived long enough to know all there is to know about life, and I certainly haven't lived long enough to tell other girls how to live their own lives. However, I believe I have lived long enough, I have seen enough, and I have been through enough to tell other girls about God, His love, His salvation, His peace, His grace, and His will and purpose for their lives.

The world throws out a lot of evil at young women everyday through radio, television, music, and music videos. Many young women fall short of Godly standards, thinking that nothing will result from their wrong actions. Of course, that is not true. The first cousin to wrong actions and behaviour is consequences. There is so much more to a young woman's life than having to always deal with consequences for wrong actions.

God wants to use you to impact this dark world, but you must first open up your heart to Him, and let Him come in and show you His divine plan for your life. That is why I wrote this book—so that young women, like you, can learn how to impact your world by being godly, pure, spirit-filled girls living on purpose for God.

That is my prayer and hope for every young woman who reads this book.

After you read this book, let me encourage you to go out and share all you have read with other girls and help them to discover God and His purpose for their lives, so that they can be "the Girl God wants", and live a great life and enjoy it.

Grace, Favor, & Blessings,

Daniella Whyte
Los Angeles, CA

.

GETTING TO KNOW THE GOD WHO WANTS YOU

God Loves You, He Really Does

If you do not get anything else from this book, I want you to know that God loves you. He really does. He loves you more than you love yourself. He loves you so much that He sent His only Son, Jesus Christ, to live, to suffer, to shed His blood, and to die a cruel death on Calvary for your sins and for mine. He loves you so much that He allowed His Son to die, so that you could live in Heaven forever with Him.

The Bible tells us in John 3:16 how much God loves us: *"For God so loved the world, that He gave His only begotten Son, that whosoever believeth in Him should not perish, but have everlasting life."* Someone asked "How much does God love us?" The reply was: "He stretched out His arms and died." That is how much God loves us and that's a whole lot of love.

In order to understand how much you need Jesus Christ, you must first **accept the fact that you are a sinner, just like me and everyone else**. Romans 3:10 says: *"There is none righteous, no, not one."* Romans 3:23 says, *"For all have sinned, and come short of the glory of God."* At one point or another in each of our lives, we have all done things that displease God and that make Him sad.

Second, **you must accept the fact that there is punishment for sin**. Romans 6:23 says: *"For the wages of sin is death."* But the good news is: *"the gift of God is eternal life through Jesus Christ our Lord."* Because we have sinned and broken God's heart, we do not deserve the gift of Heaven. In fact, we deserve death as mentioned above. God wants to save you from your sin.

Third, **you must accept the fact that Jesus is the only Somebody Who can save you.** The Bible says in Acts 4:12: *"Neither is there salvation in any other: for there is none other name under heaven given among men, whereby we must be saved."* Jesus said in John 14:6: *"I am the way, the truth, and the life: no man cometh unto the father, but by me."*

Jesus Christ, God's only Son, loves you so much that He took the pain and scorn and died a cruel death on the cross of Calvary. He bled for your sins, He was buried, and on the third day, He rose by the power of God for you and for me. The Bible says in Romans 10:9 & 13: *"That if thou shalt confess with thy mouth the Lord Jesus, and shalt believe in thine heart that God hath raised him from the dead, thou shalt be saved." "For whosoever shall call upon the name of the Lord shall be saved."*

Sister, if you believe that Jesus Christ died, was buried, and rose by the power of God for your sins, and if you want to experience the peace, love, joy, and eternal life that only Jesus Christ can give, please pray the following prayer:

Dear Jesus, I know that I am a sinner and that I have broken Your heart by breaking Your commandments. I also now know that You love me so much that you chose to die a cruel death on Calvary to save my soul. Jesus, I am sorry for all of my sins, please come into my heart right now, save my soul, and reign in my life forever. Thank You for hearing my prayer and thank You for saving me. In the name of Jesus Christ I pray. Amen.

Congratulations, on making that all important decision and I am glad that you are now a part of the Family of God.

Celebrate

Go out and buy the song, **A Sinner's Prayer** by Deitrick Haddon. As you listen to it, pray, and thank God for saving your soul. After you finish, go and tell someone else about Jesus Christ.

Think About It

"When God saves us, our sins are forgiven and forgotten forever."

"GRACE = God's Riches at Christ's Expense... And He paid full price for it."
-Walter S. Thomas

"Jesus took our place that we might have His peace; He took our sin that we might have His salvation."

Listening to the Voice of God

A lot of people think that because God is a spirit and not a human being that He does not speak to us. In a way that is true, and in a way that is not true. God does not talk to you as your best friend at school does, rather He talks to you through His Holy Word—the Bible. And that is just what this chapter is all about.

As a young lady, in order for God to speak to you, you must read, meditate on, and obey the Word of God. The Bible contains the thoughts of God.

Everything that God wants you to know about: your purpose in life, relationships, family, faith, love, the future, and anything else, is communicated to you through His Word.

Notice these three verses from the Word of God:

"Thy word is a lamp unto my feet, and a light unto my path."
—Psalm 119:105

"This book of the law shall not depart out of thy mouth; but thou shalt meditate therein day and night, that thou mayest observe to do according to all that is written therein: for then thou shalt make thy way prosperous, and then thou shalt have good success."

—Joshua 1:8

"Thy word have I hid in mine heart, that I might not sin against thee."

—Psalm 119:11

Let me encourage you to make God's Word an integral part of your life, because you will find that it will be a great source of strength and guidance to you in this world of many tempting paths. Here are some of the wonderful benefits you will receive from reading the Bible:

- ♥ It will show you God's plan for your life.
- ♥ It will give you wisdom to avoid the many traps that the world has for you.
- ♥ It will allow you to help others and to lead them to Christ.
- ♥ It will give you something positive to think about throughout the day.
- ♥ It will bless your heart and soul.
- ♥ It will guide you to great success.

Here are some things that you should do before you begin to read your Bible:

- ♥ Be humble enough to confess your sins to God. I John 1:9 says it best: *"If we confess our sins, he is faithful and just to forgive us our sins, and to cleanse us from all unrighteousness."* If you confess your sins, God will forgive you and give you a new heart and then He will be able to speak to you through His Word.

- ♥ Be ready to do what the Bible tells you. Ecclesiastes 12:13 says: *"Let us hear the conclusion of the whole matter: Fear God, and keep His commandments: for this is the whole duty of man."* God will lead you through His Word to do what is right and to do His will and plan for your life.

♥ Be willing to take His Word with you. Psalms 119:11 says: *"Thy word have I hid in mine heart, that I might not sin against thee."* The Word of God will not lead you astray. If you read it and hide it away in your heart, it will save you many heartaches and troubles because you will know what the Bible says, no matter what other people are saying or doing.

Before I go any further, let me add here, you may not be able to hear God's voice in the midst of a lot of noise and confusion, because confusion is of the devil, and God is not the author of confusion. Oftentimes, God's voice is heard as a "still small voice", in the quietness of your soul.

I really like how God revealed Himself to Elijah in I Kings 19:11-20. Here is what it says: *"And he said, Go forth, and stand upon the mount before the Lord. And, behold, the Lord passed by, and a great and strong wind rent the mountains, and brake in pieces the rocks before the Lord; but the Lord was not in the wind: and after the wind an earthquake; but the Lord was not in the earthquake: And after the earthquake a fire; but the Lord was not in the fire: and after the fire a still small voice."*

If Elijah had paid more attention to the boisterous wind, or the great earthquake, or the mighty fire, he would have missed the still, small, delicate whisper of God. So when you read your Bible, know that you are getting ready to hear the "whisper" of God. Don't pay attention to the noise. Get alone and listen to God speak.

If you do not understand something ask your parents or one of your church leaders to explain it to you. They will be happy to know that you are trying to understand the Word of God for yourself.

Never start a day without reading the Bible. Never go through a day without thinking about Its words. Never end a day without reading It again.

God loves you very much and He wants to have a very special relationship with you. In relationships, you must communicate. God is the best communicator. Love His Word and listen to It carefully, and It will never lead you astray. Lovin' the Word Always!

Get up early before anyone, when all is quiet, and get your Bible. Begin reading from any chapter, at any verse, and listen to the still, small whisper of God.

Think About It

"The problem is not that God has not spoken, but that we haven't listened."
-Max Lucado

"God speaks to those who have time to listen."

"One needs occasionally to stand aside from the hum and rush of human interests and pass on to hear the voice of God."
-Anna Julia Cooper

Prayer Power!

God loves to hear the voices of His children as they pray to Him and He longs to hear from you on a regular basis. The wonderful thing about prayer is that you don't have to hope

that your prayers get through to God and you don't have to wait in line to talk to God because He is God, and He hears your prayers night and day. David, the psalmist of the Bible said in Psalm 55:17: *"Evening, and morning, and at noon, will I pray, and cry aloud: and he shall hear my voice."*

My papa has taught me, and it has also been my personal experience that consistent calling upon God breaks through every barrier upon earth and gets to the throne of Heaven. When I do not consult with God in the morning, before I start my day, my entire day is messed up because I am trying to manage my day in my own strength.

Well, you may ask, why does God want to hear from me? God wants to hear from you for a lot of reasons. Below are just a few of them:

- ♥ God loves it when His children put their total trust in Him.

- ♥ God wants to communicate to you the things that He has in store for your life.

- God wants to bless you and provide for your needs and even your wants.

- God wants to lead you, guide you, and direct you to success, victory, and power in this life.

- God wants you to know that when everything goes down and other people go away, He will still be there to hear you and help you.

The Bible says in Jeremiah 33:3: *"Call unto me, and I will answer thee; and show thee great and mighty things which thou knowest not."* If you consistently and faithfully pray to God, He has promised that He will answer you.

Sometimes, you may feel your prayers aren't getting through to God. This is the time to pray even more. Notice these facts about prayer:

- The devil does not want you to pray because he knows that when you pray and stay in prayer, he will not be able to get you.

- The flesh does not want you to pray. Scripture says in Matthew 26:41b that *"The spirit indeed is willing, but the flesh is weak."*

- You cannot make it without prayer. When you get saved, you become attached to God, therefore, you cannot accomplish anything in your own strength. You must completely depend on the strength of God.

Sometimes, you may not feel like praying. You may not even

want to pray at a certain time. But you must learn to pray in the good times as well as in the bad times. If you ever feel like not praying, below are some tips to help you get started:

- ♥ **How to Pray**. The best way to pray is to pray like Jesus taught His disciples to pray in the Lord's Prayer (Matthew 6:9-13). If you don't want to follow a pattern, just kneel down and begin talking to God as you would your best friend. Pour out your heart to Him and have faith He hears your every word.

- ♥ **When to Pray**. Notice what the Scripture says on the first page of this chapter. That means to pray all the time. I oftentimes dive into projects and forget to pray and when things begin to go wrong, I am painfully reminded that I didn't put God in my plans. Don't make that mistake. Before you do anything—pray. Before you say anything—pray. Above all, the best time to pray is when the Holy Spirit moves you.

- ♥ **Where to Pray**. You may think that the only place to pray is in church, but that is far from true. The best place to pray is the place that you are at right now. God is everywhere at the same time. He will hear you wherever you are.

- ♥ **What to Pray**. If you do not know how to approach God, do not worry about it. Whatever you want or need or even if you just want to tell God something, it does not matter to God how you say it—just say it. My sisters and I like to pray a simple prayer. This is how it goes: "Holy Father God, it's me. Amen." This little prayer can sometimes do more than a long, wordy prayer. God honors most of all, prayers that are prayed from a sincere heart and an open spirit.

Draw close to God. Don't be discouraged if God does not answer your prayers in the time frame or in the way that you think He should. Just pray and "let go and let God." There was a song back in my grandmother's day entitled, "He's an On-Time God." Well, that is so true. "He may not come when you want Him, but He is always right on time."

Remember, "No prayer, no power. Little prayer, little power. Much prayer, much power."

Ask God to do something extraordinary for you this week, and then watch Him do it.

Think About It

"Is it possible that God wants you to be more 'selfish' in your prayers?"
            -Bruce Wilkinson

"Let prayer be our portion. Let prayer be our past-time, our passion. Let prayer be our practice."

"Your prayer on earth activates God's power in Heaven, and God's will is done on earth as it is in Heaven."
            -Max Lucado

GROWING
IN
GOD

Walking on Water: Becoming A Woman of Faith

4

*M*atthew 14:23-32 tells us of the only man beside Jesus Christ who walked on water. His name is Peter. After Peter saw Jesus walk on water, he decided that he wanted to walk on the water to make sure that it was really Jesus.

Scripture Says

"And Jesus said unto them, Because of your unbelief: for verily I say unto you, If ye have faith as a grain of mustard seed, ye shall say unto this mountain, Remove hence to yonder place; and it shall remove; and nothing shall be impossible unto you."
—Matthew 17:20

After he stepped on the water and began walking to Jesus, he took his eyes off Jesus and began looking at the winds and the waves (v. 30).

Peter forgot that Jesus was there protecting him. He forgot that Jesus was looking out for him. He forgot to exercise his faith.

So faith is kind of like walking on rough waters sometimes. In a world thwarted with depression, worry, anxiety, fret, discouragement, and fear, you've got to have faith in God to help you glide through each day.

Hebrews 11:1 says: ***"Now faith is the substance of things hoped for, the evidence of things not seen."*** Faith is trusting

God to do the impossible. What you think might be hard and what you think might never come to pass, God can make it come to pass. Always remember, "I cannot, but God can," because *"With God all things are possible"* (Matthew 19:26b).

The first key to having faith is to saturate your mind with the Word of God. Isaiah 55:11 says: *"So shall my word be that goeth forth out of my mouth: it shall not return unto me void, but it shall accomplish that which I please, and it shall prosper in the thing whereto I sent it."* Matthew 24:35 says: *"Heaven and earth shall pass away, but my words shall not pass away."* Everything that the Bible says is true, you can depend on it. If you ever feel afraid, you can comfort yourself by reading the Word of God. Let the Bible fill your mind with Its promises, and not one will return to you void.

The second key to having faith is to believe that God exists. *"But without faith it is impossible to please him: for he that cometh to God must believe that he is, and that he is a rewarder of them that diligently seek him"* (Hebrews 11:6). It takes a lot of faith to believe in God, Who you cannot see, yet Who has all power in His hands. Since God exists, it is only right that we seek His will for our lives and put all our trust in Him. He makes no mistakes about taking care of His children.

The third key to having faith is through prayer. Pray about everything. Ask God for what you need or want and He will provide it for you, guaranteed. James 1:6 says: *"But let him (her) ask in faith, nothing wavering. For he (she) that wavereth is like a wave of the sea driven with the wind and tossed."* When you pray to God, do not doubt His ability to do what you prayed about. If you doubt God that means you don't have faith.

Many people of the Bible had faith in God. Some of these people include: Abraham, Moses, Sarah, Joshua, Esther, David, and Daniel. They believed that God would do whatever He had promised to do, and they lived their lives as such. You know, it is one thing to talk about what God can do, but it is another thing to actually have the faith in Him to do as He said He would do.

One of the best definitions that I have heard of faith is this: trusting God so much to do the impossible, that you climb the tallest and biggest tree, get on the skinniest limb, and without fear, without wondering where you will land, cut the limb off behind you. You'll be surprised at where God will allow you to land. So, go on, have faith in God, and watch Him do miracles.

Think of a task that may seem impossible to accomplish this upcoming week. Pray about it. Then believe God that He can do as He promised, and will help you accomplish that task.

Think About It

"If you have the faith—God has the power."
                                        -D. L. Edwards

"Faith makes the up-look good, the out-look bright, the in-look favorable, and the future glorious."

"In order to be a cut above the rest, you have to move from passive faith to productive faith."
                                        -Walter Thomas

Obeying God with All Your Heart

5

One of the most important things that you can give to God is your obedience. He wants your total submission to His will, His Word, and His way, with all of your heart, soul, mind,

and spirit. The people who are genuinely blessed by God are the people who are genuinely obedient to God.

I really like the verse about Enoch in Genesis 5:24. It says: *"And Enoch walked with God: and he was not; for God took him."* Enoch made the decision that he was going to be completely obedient to God in his walk with God. He was so obedient that God allowed him to bypass death and go straight to Heaven.

When I say obeying God with all your mind and heart, I'm not talking about just doing things because you have to or even because your parents told you to do them. No, I am talking about doing things out of a heart-felt love for God. When you do it that way, it brings a smile to His face. 1 Samuel 15:22 says: *"...Hath the Lord as great delight in burnt offerings and sacrifices, as obeying the voice of the Lord? Behold, to obey is better than sacrifice, and to hearken than the fat of rams."* God cares more about your obeying Him than merely doing good things for Him.

If there is one thing I have learned in life, it is this—God does not want robotic service; He wants complete obedience from the heart. All throughout the Bible, you will notice that God rewards those who obey Him and punishes those who disobey Him. If you or I do wrong, God will punish us to show us that we can't keep doing the same wrong over and over again. On the other hand, if you or I obey God and keep His commandments, He will reward us with blessings and advance us to success and prosperity in life.

The main thing you can do to show God you love Him is to be totally sold-out to Him and for Him. That means whatever He tells you to do, you do it without question.

It is quite easy to say we love God, but it is harder to be totally obedient to Him.

Young girls show their obedience to God by doing the following:

♥ They accept Jesus Christ into their hearts and lives (John 3:16).

♥ They pray everyday (I Thessalonians 5:17).

♥ They read and meditate on the Word of God (Psalm 119:11).

♥ They obey and respect their parents (Ephesians 6:1-3).

♥ They go to church faithfully and surround themselves with Christians instead of those who are not saved (II Corinthians 6:14).

- ♥ They think on positive things and not on foolishness (Philippians 4:8).

- ♥ They love the Lord with all their soul (Matthew 22:37).

- ♥ They do not have sex until marriage (I Corinthians 7:1).

- ♥ They are willing to go wherever God leads them, to say whatever God tells them to say, and to do whatever God asks them to do (Isaiah 1:19).

- ♥ They learn all they can and increase in wisdom and knowledge (Proverbs 4:5-7).

How can we not obey the God of the entire universe, the God Who in His majesty thought of us before there was time? It wouldn't be right. It wouldn't be fair. So, no matter what, obey God with all your heart and mind, and He will bless your life.

Practice obedience this week. If someone in authority tells you to do something that is right, do it. You will be obeying God by obeying them.

Think About It

"No matter how fast or loudly you talk, no matter how skillfully you present your case or repeat your self-justifications, you are headed for trouble if you choose your way over God's way."
                    -Keith Butler

"Delayed obedience is disobedience."

"I know the power obedience has of making things easy which seem impossible."
                    -Teresa of Avila

Worship in Spirit and in Truth

6

*G*od loves to hear you praise Him and thank Him for all the things that He has done for you and your family because He inhabits the praise of His people.

Scripture Says
"But the hour cometh, and now is, when the true worshippers shall worship the Father in spirit and in truth: for the Father seeketh such to worship him."
—John 4:23

One of the ways that you can worship God is by going to church. Church should be a fun place to go, and not a place to pass the time, to see your friends, to pass notes, or to see who's wearing what. It should be a place to worship God. Don't play games on Sunday mornings. Be on time for church and for God. After all, isn't God on time for you?

Here are some great benefits of going to church:

- ♥ You worship God through prayer and song.

- ♥ You hear the Word of God being preached.

- ♥ You are around other Christians.

- ♥ You get to help out in various auxilaries in the church.

- ♥ You experience the presence of the Lord.

♥ You will be blessed.

Do not go to church to be seen or to see others. Go to church because you love God and you want to praise Him. Also, when you go to church, you will receive strength and encouragement for the upcoming week. Although it is good to worship God in church, you can also worship God at other places. You don't have to wait until Sunday to praise God. I like to sing praise songs in the shower, or just hum to myself while I do other work. Whatever the case, know that God accepts worship in private just as He does worship in public. He wants sincere praise from your heart.

A second way in which you can worship God is through dancing. Throughout the Bible, especially in the Psalms, you see how worship and thanksgiving were expressed through dance. II Samuel 6:14a says: *"And David danced before the Lord with all his might."* Psalm 149:3 says: *"Let them praise his name in the dance: let them sing praises unto him with the timbrel and harp."* You see, even though God knows that you love Him, He wants to see you express it. What better way to do it than through song and dance. So go ahead, sing and dance to the Lord.

One day this week, turn on some fast or slow Christian music and just sing and dance to the Lord. Show Him how much you appreciate His goodness and blessings.

Think About It

"Worship is a fresh opportunity to get to know God."
                                    -Terry Virgo

"The word 'worship' is a short form of the old word 'worthship', which means showing God the worth He holds in your life."
                                    -Tony Abram

"Without Christ's life, you can never truly worship."
                                    -Lou Giglio

How to Encourage Yourself in the Lord

Has anyone ever walked up to you and said a word of encouragement on a day when you may have needed it most? If so, didn't you feel better afterwards? Yes, we all need

encouragement at some point in our lives. But sometimes, when everyone else is sour and sad and is trying to get you discouraged, you have to be like Joshua, Caleb, and David, and keep looking to Jesus for encouragement and strength.

Do you remember in Numbers 13 and 14 when Moses sent Joshua and Caleb along with ten other men to search out the land? (Read both chapters when you get the chance.) After they searched the land and came back to the camp where Moses and the children of Israel were, the ten men gave a discouraging report. Even though the land flowed with *"milk and honey"*, and even though they brought back good fruit from the land, they chose to discourage the people from going into the land because of the *"men of a great stature"* that were there. Joshua 14:8 says that the other ten men *"made the heart of the people melt."* They discouraged the people from going into the land that God promised them.

On the other hand, Joshua and Caleb gave an encouraging report. *"And Caleb stilled the people before Moses, and said, Let us go up at once, and possess it; for we are well able to overcome it"* (Numbers 13:30). Joshua and Caleb knew about the "giants" in the land. But they also knew that God was always with them.

You see, other people around you will give a discouraging report, just like the ten men did, but you have to be like Joshua and Caleb and look on the sunny side of things and have faith that God is with you.

If you get to feeling discouraged, listen to some uplifting music. Also, pray and ask God to fill you with His joy and peace. Perhaps some of your friends are not Christians and being around them weakens your faith in God. My advice to you is, go and fellowship with other Christians and soak up the encouragement of the older women of faith, or be like David, and encourage yourself in the Lord; that is, just spend time talking to God and reading His Word.

Remember that you were made by God, chosen by God, and purposed by God for greatness. Encourage yourself in His promises.

 Write down seven things Jesus said in the Bible that really encourage your heart.

Think About It

"In the fulness of time all things
will end well."
-L.T. Burbridge

"Triumph is just 'umph'
added to try."
-Selected

"If your God is mighty enough to
ignite the sun, could it be that He is
mighty enough to light your path."
-Max Lucado

How to Obtain the Blessing and Favor of God on Your Life

*M*any young ladies think that having the blessings of God means having a big house, an expensive car, and fine clothes. That is not all that the blessings of God entails. In fact, it may

not include any of those material blessings. God may choose to bless you with peace of mind, a kind heart, and a giving spirit instead of material things.

I have noticed that the people who are genuinely happy are those who have been divinely blessed by God. You may be wondering, well, what is a blessing? A blessing is "favor bestowed upon someone or something." Has anyone ever given you something without wanting anything in return? You may say that they blessed you or showed you favor.

In order to get the blessings of God bestowed upon your life, you must do a few things:

♥ **You must be obedient to God and do His will.** Deuteronomy 11:26-28 says: *"Behold, I set before you this day a blessing and a curse; A blessing, if ye obey the commandments of the Lord your God, which I command you this day: And a curse, if ye will not*

57

obey the commandments of the Lord your God, but turn aside out of the way which I command you this day, to go after other gods, which ye have not known." Obedience is doing what He tells you to do, when He tells you to do it, without question, and sometimes, without even understanding it; for what God tells us to do is always for our good.

♥ **Meditate on the Word of God.** Joshua 1:8a says: *"This book of the law shall not depart out of thy mouth; but thou shalt meditate therein day and night..."* Being a young woman of the Word of God will save you a lot of wasted time in life. The Bible is built on facts, not feelings. If you meditate on the Word of God, you will be a smarter, wiser young woman.

♥ **You must put God above everything else.** Matthew 6:33 says: *"But seek ye first the kingdom of God, and his righteousness; and all these things shall be added unto you."* You see, a lot of people want all these things to be added unto them, but they don't want to *"seek ye first the kingdom of God."* To obtain the blessings of God, you must seek God above everything else first.

♥ **You must ask God for what you need and want.** 1 Chronicles 4:10 says: *"And Jabez called on the God of Israel, saying, Oh that thou wouldest bless me indeed, and enlarge my coast, and that thine hand might be with me, and that thou wouldest keep me from evil, that it may not grieve me! And God granted him that which he requsted."* Jabez had the right idea. Be specific in your requests.

- **You must give to others.** Matthew 10:8b says: *"...Freely ye have received, freely give."* When God blesses you in abundance, you should return the favor by being a blessing to others.

- **You must obey your parents.** Ephesians 6:1 says: *"Children, obey your parents in the Lord: for this is right."* Even if you do not understand where your parents are coming from, God still wants you to honor them and obey them. God will bless you for being obedient to your parents. That is a promise!

- **You must have faith in God.** Matthew 21:22 says: *"And all things, whatsoever ye shall ask in prayer, believing, ye shall receive."* You've got to believe that God can do the impossible. It takes strong faith to believe in a God that you cannot see; that's why it is called faith.

Follow the above seven thoughts and you will without a doubt obtain the blessings and favor of the Lord.

Get a friend and together, pray the Prayer of Jabez (1 Chronicles 4:10) each morning for a week, and watch God bless you and your friend tremendously.

Think About It

"God gives blessings to us so we can give glory to Him."

"Everything that we see is a shadow cast by that which we do not see."
-Martin Luther King, Jr.

"Without faith, nothing is possible. With it, nothing is impossible."
-Mary McLeod Bethune

ALL
THINGS
FAMILY

Love Your Family

9

*H*ave you ever heard the old proverb "Familiarity breeds contempt"? That saying is so true. It means that, oftentimes, in a family, because we know each other's weaknesses and strengths, etc., if we are not careful, we can take each other for granted.

No one has a perfect family, so it is best to love your family the way God put it together with its weaknesses and its strengths. Don't take your family for granted. They love you very much.

When your friends forsake you, oftentimes, your family will be the ones to help you and stand with you. Below are some ways in which you can love your family and help make your home, no matter how it is now, a happier home for everyone living in it:

- ♥ Treat your family the way you would want them to treat you.

- ♥ If some member of your family needs help, take the time to help them and take care of their needs.

- ♥ If you have younger brothers and sisters, take time to answer their questions and read stories to them. If they need your help, always be ready to lend a hand. They will always remember what you did for them.

♥ Do everything that you do for your family with a good attitude and spirit. I do not always feel like helping out in my family, and you won't either, but remember, it is not about feelings; it is about doing what is right, and then the good feelings will come.

♥ Plan for special events in your family, such as: family reunions, weddings, and birthdays. Help to make it an extra special time for that person.

♥ Be an encouragement to your family members. Instead of whining and complaining all the time, try to make your family members smile by saying an encouraging word, by giving them an unexpected hug, or by buying them a fashionable gift.

Doing things like these can go a long way in life. It makes for a very happy home and a lot of smiling faces. Always remember, people love to be loved.

Gather your family members on a weekday evening and read a good book aloud to them or watch an interesting movie together that appeals to adults and children alike.

Think About It

"Family happiness is homemade."

"There is nothing more truly artistic than to love people."
-Vincent van Gogh

"A love that will not bear all, care for all, share all, is not love at all."

Obeying Your Parents with All Your Heart

10

*A*s a young lady, God expects you to obey and to respect your parents. I know that sometimes when we get to a certain age, we begin to think that we know everything, even to the

point of thinking that we know more than our own parents. The truth of the matter is, we don't know more than our parents and we never will because God has fixed it that way.

Although your parents may have made some mistakes in their lives, never ever think that you are better than they are. Even though you may have more education than they were able to obtain, don't ever think that you are smarter than they are. You may have read more books and have more head knowledge, but you will never have the wisdom and years of experience that your parents have.

I remember once my Papa and I were working on the computer. Actually, we were trying to figure out how to open up a pop-up blocker program and get it firewalled. For some reason, we couldn't get it to work at first. I tried a lot of little things none of which worked. Even though I had worked on the computer more than my Papa had, and had read more than one manual on computers, my Papa was the one who knew what to do when the problem arose, because of his years of experience in life. Now, my father had never read the program manual, nor was he an expert in computers, but he knew exactly what to do, and the problem was fixed with his first instruction.

Notice what the Bible says in Ephesians 6:1-3: *"Children, obey your parents in the Lord: for this is right. Honour thy father and mother; which is the first commandment with promise; That it may be well with thee, and thou mayest live long on the earth."* No matter how old you are and no matter who your parents are, God wants you to love, respect, and obey them. If you are still under your parents' roof, you need to obey the rules of their house.

Obeying your parents is a commandment by God. It is not a suggestion. If you obey your parents, God gives a promise that you will live a prosperous, successful, and long life. Now, that is a big promise. Your flesh does not want you to be obedient, but the Holy Spirit living inside of you wants you to obey your parents with all your heart, whether you feel like it or not. I do not always "feel" like obeying my father and mother, but, I have had to learn to do what is right, whether I "feel" like it or not. I have found out that if I do what is right, the good feeling will follow.

Below are some things you can do as a young lady to help you in obeying your parents:

♥ Whatever your parents tell you to do, do it from your heart.

♥ Don't wait to be told to do what you know you ought to do. For example, if you have to wash dishes on Thursday nights, wash them without having to be told. It is a real help and blessing to your parents when you do things without having to be told.

♥ Tell your parents how much you love them and how much you appreciate all that they have done to provide for you.

♥ Take the initiative and ask your parents if you can do something that needs to be done around the house.

♥ Make a commitment to God that you will not disobey or disrespect your parents, and ask God to help you keep that commitment.

God is pleased when you obey and respect the authority that He has placed over you. Never ever disrespect or disobey your parents, and God will bless you with a long, happy, and successful life.

Celebrate

Go to your parents one day this week and tell them how much you love them and how much you appreciate them.

Think About It

"The child that never learns to obey (her) parents in the home will not obey God or man out of the home."
-Susanna Wesley

"True obedience is true freedom."
-Henry Ward Beecher

"The only safe ruler is he who has learned to obey willingly."

THE HIGH VALUE OF EDUCATION AND WISDOM

On Getting A Great Education

The spiritual part of your life is indeed the most important part of your life. Along with getting your spiritual life in order, you must also get a great education, and learn as much as you can about the world in which you live.

Sad to say, many young women think that school is a joke, that the teachers are crazy, and that books are unimportant. Thankfully, school is not that way. It is for learning new things and enhancing your mind with the history of those who have gone before you. As they say, "If you don't know where you've come from, you won't know where you are going."

It is vital to your success in life that you get a great education. Now, getting a great education does not mean rushing through books and skating through tests. To some degree it is not even about passing to the next grade. Getting a great education is about knowing that you know the material that you have been taught, and being able to use what you have learned in your everyday life.

If you study hard and strive to make good grades, you will not have a problem getting a good job, or even starting your own business. On the other hand, if you waste time in high school, you will not have the knowledge with which to go to college, and you will have a very hard time in the work world.

Sometimes, you have to choose study over having fun with your friends. If you have a big test on Friday, don't stay out all night at a party with your friends on Thursday night. You'll feel sluggish and tired on test day and you will not be able to concentrate on your test.

As you study, make sure that you study in a well-lit place in your house, or at the library. It may be hard to study when you have a lot of brothers and sisters talking, playing, and doing their own busy work around you, but you have to learn to block out all extra noises.

You must take responsibility for learning all that you can, because no one else is going to take responsibility for it.

Get a great education, no matter what it takes or what obstacles you have to overcome, and you will come out the better and stronger for it.

Do you have a subject that you are struggling with in school? If so, take that subject and spend extra time studying it. Tell yourself that you can learn it and then do it.

Think About It

"Nothing we learn in this world is
ever wasted."
-Eleanor Roosevelt

"Learning is not attained by
chance. It must be sought for with
ardor and attended to with
diligence."
-Abigail Adams

"Asking questions is not silly."
-African Proverb

Reading to Enrich your Life

12

$\mathcal{R}$eading is very important if you want to advance in life very fast. Good books can put you head and shoulders above your peers. It can take you places mentally, that physically,

you may not be able to go. I encourage you to read good, wholesome books and materials whenever and wherever you can.

Mind you, everything that has the "Read Me" sign on it is not necessarily good reading material. So, as you make your reading selections, watch what you pick. Books that have sexually explicit language in them, or other ungodly language is not good for you because it will corrupt your mind. The Bible says in 1 Corinthians 15:33 to: ***"Be not deceived: evil communications corrupt good manners."***

The very best book to read is the Bible—the Word of God. The Bible contains the thoughts of God and His plans for His children if they obey Him. It has everything that you need to know about life, faith, family, friendships, sex, relationships, love, joy, righteous living, and anything else you might want to know.

Before you go to pick out other books, read the Bible first. It will help you make the right choices in your reading life.

Include in your reading list, books about your favorite countries, your favorite food, or even your favorite hobby. Read a history book about America and about the world, in general. You will be surprised at how much knowledge you will gain.

Well, you may ask why all this emphasis on reading? The truth is, many people do not like to read. Below are three reasons why I believe reading is important:

- ♥ Reading makes you think. Television does not. People who don't think don't get anywhere in life, because they constantly depend on others to think for them. One of my Papa's mottos is: "Pray, Think, Do."

- ♥ Reading good books can take you into another good world.

- ♥ Reading gives you an advantage over those who don't read. Reading gives you a bigger picture of the world and a broader foundation of knowledge. While reading, you can increase your vocabulary as well.

Now that you know what to read, what not to read, and how reading helps you in life, below are a few tips on how to read:

- ♥ Set a goal of reading at least three books a month and stick to that goal.

- ♥ Read with an open mind. Read so that what you read becomes a part of you and it doesn't just go in one side of your brain and right out the other.

- ♥ Read to remember. What you read in a book will come

back to your mind one day, and you can implement it into what you are doing or saying at that time.

♥ Practice what you read. There is a saying that goes like this, "What goes into a mind, comes out in a life." If you feed on positive things, you will do positive things. However, if you feed on negative things, you will do negative things. In other words, what you read influences your life.

It is sad to see so many teenage girls bored with school and bored with life. It is even sadder to see them live purposeless lives with their minds dulled by television, the internet and videos. Get away from that stuff. Get away from what negative people are doing around you and get into a good book. It will make all the difference in your life.

Create a book club and invite the kids in your neighborhood to your house (with your parent's permission), once a week, provide some snacks, and pick a good book to read to the kids who come.

Think About It

"To read without reflecting is to cram the intellect and paralyze the mind."
-S.E. Wesson

"Life-transforming ideas have always come to me through books."
-Bell Hooks

"Reading is to the mind what exercise is to the body."
-Joseph Addison

The Value of Obtaining Wisdom

13

*T*his matter of obtaining wisdom is very crucial to success in life because oftentimes, you can keep yourself out of a lot of trouble if you just use a little wisdom.

There are a lot of things that you may know how to do, but if you do not know why you are doing those things, there is no use in doing them. That is where wisdom comes in. King Solomon, the wisest man who ever lived said in Proverbs 8:11: *"For wisdom is better than rubies; and all the things that may be desired are not to be compared to it."* Wisdom is not stuck up. It does not behave itself unwisely. It thinks for itself. It knows why it is doing something. In other words, it knows the purpose and results of the things that it is doing. Wisdom is not just a hearer of truth, but a doer of truth.

Now, you cannot get true wisdom from books, or yoga, or by studying. True wisdom comes from God. You have to ask Him for it. James 1:5 tells us that: *"If any of you lack wisdom, let him ask of God, that giveth to all men liberally, and upbraideth not; and it shall be given him."*

King Solomon prayed and asked God for wisdom above silver, gold, fine things and other riches. True wisdom comes from

God, and if you have the faith to ask God for wisdom, He will give it to you.

The wonderful wisdom that God gives can open up your eyes to see many things that you may not otherwise be able to see. It helps you to deal with tough situations which may, otherwise, be difficult to deal with. Wisdom is about being able to make the right decisions at any given time. So, please ask God for wisdom and His wisdom will guide you to a great life that you will enjoy.

Write down seven questions to ask one of the older women in your church. Set up an appointment with her, like on a Sunday afternoon. Be a sponge and soak up the knowledge, advice, and wisdom that she gives you.

Think About It

"True wisdom starts with a heart full of faith, not a head full of facts."

"Wisdom is the supreme part of happiness."

-Sophocles

"Common sense is instinct; enough of it is genius."

IT'S ALL ABOUT PURPOSE AND PASSION

Discovering Your Destiny

14

$\mathcal{G}$od has given each person born into this world a destiny—a purpose to fulfill for His glory. Charles Wesley put it this way in his beautiful hymn, "A charge to keep I have; a God to glorify." God did not cause you to be born to just take up space. He made you to do something with your life that will count, that will help other people, and that will glorify Him.

> **Scripture Says**
>
> "So God created man in his own image, in the image of God created he him; male and female created he them."
> —Genesis 1:27

God has also given each person, including you, certain talents to fulfill their purpose. Now, there are some people who use the talents that God has given them for their own selfish gains. God wants you to use your talents and gifts for His glory.

Jesus told His disciples a parable on the Mount of Olives in Matthew 25:14-29 about a man who called his three servants and gave them each talents, according to their abilities. He gave one servant five talents, the other he gave two talents, and the last received one talent. The first two servants went and invested their talents and got double what they had before. The last servant went and hid his talent in the ground and gained nothing from doing so. The lesson is that if you use the "talents" and gifts that God has given you, He will bless you with more.

Discovering your purpose is simply discovering what God wants you to do with your life. Once you find that out, you must pursue it with all of your might, according to His will.

In order to find out your destiny, the first thing that you must do is pray. Pray for God's leadership and guidance in doing His will. Then, you must read the Bible daily. Also be ready for any opportunity God may give to you to enhance your skills and talents even more. Don't squander the talents that God has given you as the last servant did in the parable. Instead, use them in any way that you can. Don't let anyone talk you out of doing what God wants you to do with your life. Fulfill your purpose and reach your destiny!

Pray everyday and ask God what He wants you to do with your life. After He tells you, go out and celebrate, and then learn all you can so that you can be the best that you can be for God.

Think About It

"It is not what man does that determines whether his work is sacred or secular, it is why he does it."

-A.W. Tozer

"In the long run men hit only what they aim at."

-Henry David Thoreau

"Strive to make something of yourself; then strive to make the most of yourself."

-Alexander Crummell

Living On Purpose

15

*M*any books have been written on this very important subject—living on purpose. It is a subject that many people talk about, but it is also something that many people are not doing.

Scripture Says

"The thief cometh not, but for to steal, and to kill, and to destroy: I am come that they might have life, and that they might have it more abundantly."
—John 10:10

It troubles me to see many young women, go through life without knowing why they were put here, without any direction and drive, and without giving anything back to their communities to make the world a better place in which to live. These dear people just meander through life doing the same mundane, and quite frankly, boring things everyday. These people have no excitement in their lives. They have nothing to look forward to in the mornings or throughout the day.

Therefore, they live, work, and die in total obscurity, without having contributed one good thing to society. This is very sad, indeed. God wants you to know that as a young lady, He put you on this earth to do something great for Him. Here are three things that God has given to you, and to you only:

♥ God has given you a life that only you can live. No one else can live your life for you.

- God has given you talents, skills, and abilities that only you have. No one can do what you can do the exact way that you can do it. You are a unique creation. God does not make duplicates.

- God has given you a creative mind to conceive new ideas and bring them into being, just as He conceived the idea of this earth and brought it into existence. Since you are made in the image of God, you are to be like Him. I believe since God "created" something, He made you to "create" as well. Now, you may be asking, how can I begin to live my life on purpose and to its fullest? Notice what the Bible says in John 10:10b: *"...I am come that they might have life, and that they might have it more abundantly."*

- You must find out what your natural gifts and talents are and begin to use them with all your might. Jesus said in Luke 19:10: *"For the Son of man is come to seek and to save that which was lost."* In this verse, Jesus is clearly stating His purpose for coming to earth. Whatever you can do well, be it singing, dancing, hairstyling, babysitting, or making chocolate sundaes, you need to do it to the best of your ability. On the other hand, if there are things that you feel uncomfortable doing, or that you simply cannot do, don't waste your time or other people's time pursuing those things. You will feel out of place, and will mess up the job. Right now, my purpose is to write this book to you and to encourage you in God's love. I would not be fulfilled if I were not doing this at this time.

- You must be humble. God honors humility. Luke 14:11

tells us: *"For whosoever exalteth himself shall be abased; and he that humbleth himself shall be exalted."* God loves people who are humble. You will not get far in this life with a proud spirit.

♥ Do not follow the crowd. I once read this sign on a billboard: "Some may, but you cannot." There are some good things that God may not want you to do because He has not given you the ability with which to do it. Don't follow the crowd. You have to be honest with yourself and do the things that you know you have the talent to do. Be your own person and think for yourself.

♥ You must be determined. Living on purpose requires a made-up mind. Determination automatically sets you apart from those who want to live the boring, mundane life, because you have a goal and have something exciting to look forward to. Determination clears doubt from your mind because no one can stop a made-up mind.

Take a moment to pray and ask God what did He create you to do. Be still and silent and listen very closely for His reply, because He will answer you. Your ultimate purpose is to touch the lives of others around you for the better, to make a difference in your society, and to help heal the wounds of suffering humanity. Don't live the boring life that millions of people live everyday. Live for something! "Stand for something, or you will fall for anything!" Be excited about your purpose, your goal, and your destiny, and live a life on purpose for God's glory.

Find out what you enjoy doing. Then be innovative and create new ways of doing the things you love.

Think About It

"Life without passion is unforgivable."
-Sean John

"I'm not here just to make a living, I'm here to make a difference."
-Helice Bridges

"Everyone has his own specific vocation in life...Therein he cannot be replaced nor can his life be repeated. Thus, everyone's task is as unique as is his specific opportunity to implement it."
-Victor Frankl

Big Dreams Are a Big Deal

16

I believe that one of the main reasons so many young women don't get ahead in life is because they do not know the value of setting goals and sticking with their dream. Dreams are a big deal, but fulfilling those dreams is an even bigger deal. In order to fulfill your dreams, you must set some clearly defined goals. For example, if your dream is to go to college right out of high school, you can fulfill that dream, if you set clear goals for yourself and stick to them. It also will take perseverance, determination, and hard work to accomplish what you set out to do.

Scripture Says
"And Joseph dreamed a dream, and he told it his brethren: and they hated him yet the more."
—Genesis 37:5

Now, let me define for you what a "goal" is. A goal is something worthy of being pursued. Goals consist of looking out into the future and mapping out the things that you want to accomplish in your life.

Mind you, I am not talking about getting a car, getting a job, and making money; everybody says they want to do that. I am talking about being the first woman president or building your own hospital for sick children in Africa or creating the next new energy-saving car model. Goals are things that change your life and change the lives of others for the better.

Anything that you want to do for God and for the enhancement of society is a worthy goal.

Achievement of worthy goals takes creativity, perseverance, courage, grace, strength, falling down and getting back up again, a tough hide, and a will to stick and stay no matter what. Here are a few things to think about as you set your goals:

- ♥ Do your goals acknowledge God? As a Christian young woman, God doesn't want you to do anything that is out of His will. Check your goals and see if you have taken thought to include God in your plans.

- ♥ Are your goals your goals? I know it is an odd question. But, what I mean is, are you setting the goals for yourself, or are you letting other people set goals for you? If you are, you are not going to enjoy your life the way you should, because you are allowing someone else to dictate to you what they think you should be doing. Let me add here: you should seek the advice of your parents because they know what is in you and what you are capable of doing.

- ♥ Do your goals include contributing to worthy causes? You can be a blessing to other people, if you set goals that help with worthy programs. And by the way, you will receive a blessing yourself.

- ♥ Are you willing to discipline yourself to reach your goals? Anybody who has ever accomplished anything in life knows that discipline is the key.

♥ Can you dream big? Can you think outside of this world? Can you imagine doing things that no one else has done before? Can you see the big picture of your life?

Once you set your goals, pray over them daily and then pursue them. Don't stop until you accomplish them, and don't let anyone stop you.

Make a list of all the things you want to accomplish with your life. After doing so, pray over them and set goals that will help you accomplish them. When you reach a goal, reward yourself and then push on to the next one.

Think About It

"Recognize the power you have to choose your actions, your responses, and the direction of your life."
                        -Valorie Burton

"A vision doesn't turn into a reality without a price."
                        -Eddie L. Long

"Don't sit down and wait for opportunities to come; you have to get up and make them."
                        -Madame C.J. Walker

PURITY IS
YOUR POWER

The Hidden Power of Purity

17

*I*t is important for young women to live a pure life, especially in today's society, with so many roads that lead to sex and destruction, and a society where women who are of impure hearts and behavior are placed in very low esteem. It is not going to be easy living a pure life in an impure world, but God wants pure young women who are living for Him and not for the world.

> **Scripture Says**
> "...Keep thyself pure."
> —1 Timothy 5:22

Below are some things to keep in mind regarding this all important subject of purity:

- ♥ Purity begins in the heart. Matthew 5:8 says: *"**Blessed are the pure in heart: for they shall see God.**"* If we get our heart right and begin exercising the fruits of the spirit—love, joy, peace, patience, kindness, goodness, faithfulness, gentleness and self-control, then we are well on our way to having a pure heart. We should pray daily to God to create within us a pure heart and to give us the mind of Christ.

- ♥ Purity is a lifestyle. Yes, it is a way of living. God calls us to be holy or pure in our lifestyle. ***"Be ye holy for I am holy."***

- ♥ Purity is a choice, and a choice worth making. Those

who choose to live a pure life, by the power of the Holy Spirit, and as unto the Lord, will be richly blessed for doing so and will avoid much heartache in life. Once you make that decision to live a lifestyle of purity, certain things will become second nature to you, like being honest and keeping your word.

♥ Purity shines even in the dark. Even if all the other girls are living impure lives and seem to be getting all the attention, it will not last long. In the end, if you maintain a life of purity, you will stand out in the crowd.

♥ Purity brings joy and freedom. It's almost impossible to be joyful and free if you have a lot of sin weighing you down. If you really want joy and freedom on the inside, you must commit to living a pure life.

No matter what, be pure in your thoughts, be pure in your actions, be pure in your speech, be pure in what you read, and be pure in what you view on television or on the internet. Purity will take you a long way.

 Create a little party with brownies and lemonade. Gather two girlfriends and the three of you make a commitment to God to stay pure and holy for His glory.

Think About It

"In pursuing a lifestyle of purity there is so much freedom."
-Joshua Harris

"I feel very strongly that without Jesus it is not possible to live a lifestyle of purity."
-Kaye Briscoe King

"Purity is governed by its value."
-Dannah Gresh

The Real Deal About Sex

18

It pains me to hear the world tell young women to "wrap it up," "that it's okay to have sex," "nothing is going to happen," "all you have to do is use a condom," "sex outside of marriage is okay," etc. Because of these lies that the devil and the world are telling young women, which many are falling for, so many have lost their virginity by having sex before marriage, and many are living with the pain, the embarrassment, and the hurt that comes with it.

> **Scripture Says**
>
> "Flee fornication. Every sin that a man doeth is without the body; but he that committeth fornication sinneth against his own body."
> —1 Corinthians 6:18

I hate to tell you, but sex is not about "the birds and the bees." Babies don't come from storks. A woman's stomach doesn't become bigger by osmosis. This whole "mystery" as to where babies come from and what sex is, etc, is very simple. Babies come from a male and a female getting together and having sex. The woman gets pregnant and that is how the baby comes into existence.

Sex was created by God so that more people could come into being and populate the earth. Now you see, there is no "dirty little secret" to uncover. Here are five lies that the devil is telling young women about sex and why you shouldn't believe them:

107

- ♥ **Everyone's doing it.** First, everyone is not doing it. Statistics show that 50% of the girls between 15 and 19 have had sex already. You know what? That means that there are still 50% between 15 and 19 who haven't had sex yet. So, that means that everyone's not doing it.

- ♥ **Sex is a mystery.** Sex is not a mystery. God only has one pre-requisite for sex, and that is, it is to be done in the circle of marriage to protect all the people involved and to keep you back from a lot of pain.

- ♥ **Sex was created by the devil.** Sex was not created by the devil. Sex was created by God.

- ♥ **"Safe sex" is safe.** The only "safe sex" is sex within the confines of marriage. Sex outside of marriage will bring shame, hurt, and pain to everyone involved. This is what happens when people disobey God.

- ♥ **You've got to experiment with sex.** No! You do not have to experiment with sex. When and if God wants you to get married, that is the time for you to experience sex with your husband because then it will be right and it will feel right.

Let me now take the opportunity to tell you the real deal about sex: (1) At this stage in your life, sex is not important. In fact, sex should not be on your mind in the slightest. (2) In a life time, sex takes up only about one percent of your life. (3) Do not let a few minutes of pleasure ruin the other ninety-nine percent of your life. (4) Think of the embarrassment that you will go through by having sex outside of marriage and possibly getting pregnant.

Don't believe the devil's lies because he likes to take God's simple truths and twist them.

Find a quiet place and study 1 Corinthians chapter 6 and 7. After that make a journal about what purity means to you. Make a commitment to God to not have sex until you are married.

Think About It

"There is a dull, monotony, sheer boredom in all of life when virginity and purity are no longer prized. By trying to grab fulfillment everywhere, we find it nowhere."
-Elisabeth Elliot

"Your disobedience does not remove God from your life. It does remove God's blessing from your life."
-Tim Cook

"Sex involves not just the sexual organs, but also the heart..."
-Kristine Napier

The Value of Remaining a Virgin until You Get Married

19

Contrary to what the world and maybe your friends might be telling you, staying a virgin is cool. It is not only cool, it is worth it. Having sex before marriage is not cool and it may be fun while you are doing it, but it will not be fun when you have to face the consequences. The devil will also try to tell you that sex is what is missing in your life. Don't believe him. Nothing is missing in your life if you have Jesus Christ.

Below are some reasons why it is important to protect your virginity and stay pure for Jesus Christ and for your future soulmate:

♥ God said so. This is the most important reason. God wants you to have a happy life, and since He created you, He knows what's best for you.

♥ You won't be happy if you do otherwise. Sex outside of marriage brings pain and heartache.

♥ You can contract sexually transmitted diseases and/or AIDS.

♥ You could get pregnant outside of the protection of marriage.

♥ You would not be a good role model. What an example to set for other young girls! You never know who is watching you, so be a good example to others.

Here are some ways that you can protect your virginity and purity for God:

♥ Make up your mind **now** to remain a virgin until marriage. Sometimes, you have to just make up your mind to do right even though no one else is doing right, and not to do wrong even though everyone may be doing wrong. It was Cicero who said: "A life of peace, purity, and refinement leads to a calm and untroubled old age." Keeping your virginity is important to a life of peace and no regrets.

♥ Don't stare at boys. Proverbs 4:25 says: *"Let thine eyes look right on, and let thine eyelids look straight before thee."* If you stare at boys, they will think that you like them or something, and they will think that that is an open door for them to approach you in a disrespectful manner.

♥ Do not carry on a conversation with a boy or a man. Some are slick and can possibly talk you into doing something you will regret.

♥ Don't hang around bad places and bad people. Many young women have gotten into a lot of trouble by doing this. The people and places you hang around can have a powerful influence on you, be it negative or positive.

♥ Set high biblical standards. Don't follow the "standards" of the world. The world's standard is "Anything goes." So, set your own standards of purity and holiness according to the Bible and live by them.

God is looking for pure young women who are willing to stand for Him in this wicked world. You can become a part of God's army by protecting your virginity from the devil and evil boys. You will feel good and free if you do it God's way and there are people in the world who will pretty soon follow you. Keeping your virginity is cool.

Celebrate

Study what it means to be a virgin and stay pure in an impure world. Next Sunday, wear an all-white outfit and during prayer time, go to the altar and promise God that you will remain a virgin until marriage.

Think About It

"The Bible has a word to describe 'safe sex': It's called marriage."
-Gary Smalley & John Trent

"Sex is so beautiful, it is worth protecting."
-Josh McDowell

"Be sure you put your feet in the right place, and then stand firm."
-Abraham Lincoln

The Truth About Boys

20

*W*e have all heard of the wonderful, fairy-tale stories where a spell is broken, the prince finds the princess and sweeps her off her feet, and takes her to a castle and they live happily ever after. Well, those stories are great, but those days of princes and princesses are long gone so let me tell you the truth about boys:

♥ Boys are more aggressive than girls. That is the way God made them and because of this, oftentimes, they will try to make a move to get you to do what they want you to do.

♥ Many boys think negatively about girls. Due to the behavior of some young women, society has viewed women in a negative light. You do not have to be viewed in this way. If you carry yourself in a respectful and dignified manner, generally speaking, boys and society will think differently of you.

♥ My papa has taught me that boys' minds are stimulated by sight more than anything else in the beginning. Unlike God who looks at the heart, boys look at the outward appearance.

♥ Oftentimes, boys really don't think you mean "NO", when you say "NO". Do not act timid and unsure of what you stand for. Say "NO" with boldness and with conviction and with a straight face, and they will respect you and leave you alone. Or, they may respect you enough to ask your hand in marriage, one day.

♥ In this "free-love" society, many boys think they can get you without much effort. It is up to you to let them know that you are not that type of young lady. You should have the conviction and make the commitment, that there will be no touching, kissing, or hugging whatsoever until you marry.

Don't give in to the pressures of the guys around you, Christian or not. Instead, give in to holiness and righteousness and let God direct you in your relationships. Romans 8:6 says: *"For to be carnally minded is death; but to be spiritually minded is life and peace."*

Remember, "boys will be boys". You do not have to give in to them under any circumstances whatsoever. Focus on your studies and on your life goals because you do not need a boy to live a fulfilled life.

Celebrate

Go to the store and buy yourself individually wrapped chocolate candy or whatever candy you like. With each bite, think of how many things you can do for God in your young life if you don't get bogged down with impure living and boys.

Think About It

"Where modesty is absent virtue has no means of protection."
-Unknown

"Only chastity and self-respect can bring true love."
-Juanita Bynum

"Love will always endure if you keep it pure."
-Unknown

To Date or Not to Date

21

In my few years on this earth, during which I have had the privilege of reading the entire Bible, from cover to cover, (I suggest you do it as well), I have not read any specific verses from the Bible in regards to dating. Now, I have never been on a date, and I am not an expert on dating, but for those of you who do date, below are some biblical principles that you might want to consider:

> ## Scripture Says
> "But as he which hath called you is holy, so be ye holy in all manner of conversation; Because it is written, Be ye holy; for I am holy."
> --1 Peter 1:15-16

♥ Make sure that your date is a Christian and that he has a growing relationship with God. If he does not, you are already headed for trouble. The Bible says in 2 Corinthians 6:14: *"Be ye not unequally yoked together with unbelievers; for what fellowship hath righteousness with unrighteousness? and what communion hath light with darkness?"* If both you and your date love God and want to please Him over yourselves, you will keep the relationship in line with God's Word.

♥ Make it clear to your date that sex before marriage is not an option. In my opinion, dates are for people who are mature and who are serious about marriage. It is not for fooling around.

♥ Make a commitment to God before you go on your date to keep your relationship pure and holy before Him. That includes no hugging and touching, etc. First Peter 1:16b says: *"...Be ye holy; for I am holy."* Before you go on your date, pray with your date, in the presence of your parents, for guidance.

♥ While on your date, ask questions. That's what dates are for—to get to know each other. But, don't discuss sex or marriage on your date? Why? Because if you do, both you and your date, will be more focused on fulfilling your own desires and will make controlling those desires harder.

♥ Communicate purity to your date, not only in body, but also in your language, your spirit, and your actions. Doing that will help set a Godly standard for your relationship.

♥ Never date alone. If possible, go with a group or even with your parents, for accountability's sake.

In closing, let me remind you that dating is not a sin. There is nothing wrong with it. But, if you do not do it God's way and you allow your feelings to get tangled up in your date, that can and will get you into a lot of trouble. So, before you go on a date, pray and ask God to guide you. Let your parents help you. Keep your dating life open to them and be honest with them about it. Let your parents meet your date and if he does not meet their approval get rid of him. Your parents know what is best for you. In my opinion, it is really best not to date at all. Have you ever read the book, *I Kissed Dating Goodbye* by Joshua Harris? Before you go on another date, I suggest you read it.

Keep this verse in mind: ***"Whatsoever ye do in word or deed, do all in the name of the Lord Jesus"*** (Colossians 3:17a).

Gather four friends together, and see if they would be interested in joining you in "Kissing Dating Goodbye." Read the book, *I Kissed Dating Goodbye*, by Joshua Harris.

Think About It

"Integrity means having a conscience and listening to it."
-Arthur Gordon

"Character is much easier kept than recovered."
-Thomas Paine

"The time is always right to do what is right."
-Martin Luther King, Jr.

WALKING ON A HIGHER PLANE

What's Love Got to do with It?

22

We all need someone to love us and show us that we are loved. In her song, "What's Love Got to do with It?" Tina Turner discusses love as an emotion rather than a choice. She portrays love as something that people can do without. Through the song, you get the sense that love is something that you can turn off and turn on whenever you feel like it.

> **Scripture Says**
> "We love him, because he first loved us."
> -1 John 4:19

Fortunately, true love is not an emotion, rather it is a choice-a powerful choice. God, the originator of love, is our greatest example of true love. His love is an unconditional love. This love is pure, and Christ-like. It is that way regardless of what we do or say because God never changes and His love for His children never changes.

So, really, "what's love got to do with it"? It has a whole lot to do with it. God sent His Son, Jesus Christ, to die a cruel death on Calvary for your sins and my sins. Then, He was buried, and early Sunday morning, He got up out of the tomb, conquering death for you and me, so that we could have eternal life. Jesus sacrificed Himself for us. That's true love.

So many girls go out into the world to try to find someone to love them. Unfortunately, they get tangled up in this web called love and mess up their lives for a very long time. It ends up that way because they do not understand that God is the only Person Who can love them for them and love them unconditionally. True love does not depend on what you do, or who you are; true love is the love that keeps on loving no matter what.

So, here is how you can experience the unconditional, agape love of God in your life, all of the time:

> ♥ Fall in love with Jesus Christ. Fall in love with His words and with communicating to Him your needs. Stay in close contact with God, *"For he hath said, I will never leave thee, nor forsake thee"* (Hebrews 13:5b). You can go to God with any problem, any frustration, or any situation, and He will hold out His arms to you, every time.

> ♥ Let God be in control of your life. He loves you so much, that He does not want you to make wrong decisions or bad choices. John 1:3 says: *"All things were made by him; and without him was not anything made that was made."* God should not just be a part of our lives, He should be our lives, and He should control our lives. After all, our life is in His hands. Right? He will work everything out for our good - even

the bad stuff. *"All things work together for the good to them that love God"* (Romans 8:28a).

♥ Share God's love with others. Jesus Christ commands us throughout the Bible, to tell others about His love and grace. One of the greatest feelings in the world comes when we share the love of God with others. We can express God's love to other people by showing them how to be saved. It is also important to love and care for other people ourselves. John 13:35 says: *"By this shall all men know that ye are my disciples, if ye have love one to another."* We are to love those who we like and even those we may dislike, because loving them will make the difference.

Love is a choice, and as humans, we are not naturally loving. But God is, because *"God is love"* (I John 4:8b). Maybe we should ask the question, "What's God's love got to do with it?" The answer is everything.

Think of someone who is going through a hard time. Whisper a prayer for her, then call her up on the phone, tell her how much you love her, and see what you can do to lighten her load.

Think About It

"Love is not based on a person's intelligence or state of life, but rather on the size of the heart."
-Author Unknown

"God loves His girls, not because of who they are, but because of Who He is."

"God loves each of us as if there were only one of us."
-St. Augustine

Be a Tough-Minded Teen

As a young woman, you must learn to be strong and tough-minded. If you do not live your life based upon biblical facts, this crazy world will knock you down, run you over, and you will be left to get up all by yourself.

Scripture Says
"Therefore, my beloved brethren, be ye stedfast, unmoveable, always abounding in the work of the Lord, forasmuch as ye know that your labour is not in vain in the Lord."
--1 Cor. 15:58

You probably know some girls who whine and cry about everything and who do not know how to take "no" for an answer. You don't want to be like that.

Being tough-minded does not mean being so serious that you don't laugh and you cannot be nice to other people. It doesn't mean that you can't have a good time. It simply means paying attention to what you are doing, not believing what everybody says, and sucking some things up and taking responsibility for yourself and your behaviour. Here are some things that will help you to be tough-minded and live a successful and unhindered life:

♥ Have a plan for your life. If you don't, somebody else will plan your life for you.

♥ Think for yourself. If you know or even think something is wrong, don't do it, even if everyone else is doing it.

♥ Pray and read your Bible daily. Before you do anything, no matter how small it is, pray and ask God to bless it. If you don't, the devil will mess your day up. I know, I have seen him do it. Meditate on the Word of God.

♥ Don't allow yourself to get into trouble. Even if all your girlfriends are doing it, you don't do it. In fact, try to help them not to get into trouble. Don't do things that will make God sad and hurt your conscience.

♥ Be on time. Have a schedule and be on time for everything.

♥ Be organized. Disorganized people waste the most time and lose the most money because they always have to look for things. Know where your belongings are and keep everything in its place.

♥ Don't lie. Lying can mess you up very much, and very fast. My father told me once, "Nobody is worth lying to and nothing is worth lying about." Just keep it real and people will always trust you, depend on you, and give you anything you want. Jesus said: *"the truth shall set you free."*

♥ Learn all you can. Be a sponge. Soak up good knowledge from books and school. You must learn about the world around you so that you won't get left behind.

♥ Always have something to do. If you sit around staring into space, people are going to think you are crazy. Find out what you like to do then do it with all your might.

♥ Live based on truth and facts. If we all lived based on lies and on how we feel, we would live a very unhappy life. You've got to deal with reality. I think Fantasia Barrino said it best: "Life is not a fairy tale."

I know, it's tough to be tough-minded, but if you make up your mind to be tough-minded, you can save yourself a lot of valuable time, energy, bad grades, disrespect, headache, and money. Be tough-minded and live a very happy, peaceful, and stress-free life. It's that important.

Celebrate

Go out and buy a daily planner. Each day ask God what would He have you to do that day. Write it down in your planner and strive to accomplish it all. Also, make a commitment to God and to your parents that you won't whine and complain when you can't have your way.

Think About It

"The only reconstruction worthwhile is a reconstruction of thought."
-Kelly Miller

"I see the potential to make a difference. And I get the courage to break away from the crowd."
-Michael Tait

"Mental toughness is to physical as four is to one."
-Bobby Knight

Sacrifice

One of the greatest sacrifices that you can make is to touch and change someone's life for the better, by using the resources that God has given you. After all, that is what Jesus did. He

made the greatest sacrifice ever. When you see someone in need, you should help him or her, if the Lord leads you to, and if you have the resources to do so. Even if you have to give up something that you love, you will feel better that you did. Never get too proud and start thinking that you are better than anyone else, to the point, that you can't stop and help someone.

Notice these verses in Proverbs 11:24-25: *"There is that scattereth, and yet increaseth; and there is that withholdeth more than is meet, but it tendeth to poverty. The liberal soul shall be made fat: and he that watereth shall be watered also himself."*

Those who freely give to others and help others in need, without expecting the favor to be returned, will be greatly blessed by God. When you help other people, even if your resources are small, you show them how much God loves them through you. Matthew 25:40 says: *"...Inasmuch as ye have done unto one of the least of these my brethren, ye have done it unto me.*" Do not reject those who need your help. If you do, you are rejecting Jesus Christ. This verse tells us that helping people in need, like feeding the hungry, clothing the naked, and housing the homeless, or even giving school supplies away to another kid who needs them, is like doing it to Jesus Christ.

Here are some areas that you may be able to make some sacrifices in for other people. If you can't find a way to help someone in one of the ways listed below, try to think of your own:

♥ Go to a hospital and pray with and for a sick person.

♥ If you see someone looking sad, go up to her, pat her on the back, and tell her, "It's going to be okay."

♥ Volunteer at a daycare center.

♥ Volunteer at your local homeless shelter.

♥ Give a hug.

♥ Smile. It can make someone's day brighter.

♥ Sponsor a Third World child through World Vision or some other charitable organization.

♥ Donate your outgrown clothes to a thrift store or to a person who you know needs them.

♥ Read a few books a week to an elementary school child.

♥ Mentor a troubled child.

♥ Help out at your church.

Do without some things for a while, so that other people can have the joy of having those same things. God wants to use you in a great way. What better way than to let Him know that you are an open vessel available for His use. Always have your eyes open for opportunities to help. You may never know how great an impact something you did, that you thought was small, can be.

Give up something that you really love in order to help and be a blessing to someone who could benefit from it.

Think About It

*"Let no one ever come to you without
leaving better and happier."*
-Mother Teresa

*"Life's most urgent question is:
What are you doing for others."*
-Martin Luther King, Jr.

*"What do we live for if not to
make the world less difficult
for each other?"*
-George Eliot

On Being Truly Happy

25

A happy person is pleasant to be around. Nobody wants to be around a sad and gloomy person. If you are unhappy around other people, you can make them feel miserable, too, especially if they are the type of people who are easily influenced by others.

> **Scripture Says**
> "Rejoice in the Lord alway: and again I say, Rejoice."
> --Philippians 4:4

Jesus Christ commands us to be cheerful. He says in John 16:33b: *"...In this world ye shall have tribulation: but be of good cheer; I have overcome the world."* It really hurts God when His children, who He has done so much for, walk around being and looking sad and grumpy.

If you are happy in Jesus Christ, even your problems cannot make you sad, especially if you believe His Word that says: *"Casting all your cares upon him for he careth for you."* Do you know the story of "Pollyanna"? Pollyanna was a sunshiny child, even around one of her always sad and grumpy family members, and she always made other people smile. One day, she was climbing a tree and she missed her step, fell, and broke her leg. A couple of days later, when she was in the hospital, she told her family this: "I'm so happy I broke my leg." Even though Pollyanna had a broken leg and had to walk with a crutch for the remainder of her life, she remained happy in spite of her condition.

No matter what happens in your life, God wants you to be happy and to show your happiness to other people, because, surprisingly, your happiness can make other people happy. Wherever you are and whatever you are doing, be happy.

Now, you are not going to feel like being cheerful or feel like smiling all the time. I don't always feel like being cheerful. Sometimes, I feel like being sad and grumpy. I have to keep reminding myself, it is not about feelings, it is about doing right, and I have learned that if I choose to do right the good feelings come.

Abraham Lincoln said a long time ago that "people are about as happy as they make up their minds to be." Happiness is a choice. At the same time, nothing or nobody can make you sad, unless you let them. Doing things is not going to make you happy if you were not already happy before you did those things. If you make the choice in your heart to be happy on the inside, that happiness will show on the outside.

There is a song that has a line in it that goes like this: *"This joy I have, the world didn't give it to me. The world didn't give it, and the world can't take it away."* If you make the choice to be happy in Jesus Christ, nothing or nobody can take it away.

Practice smiling and having a happy spirit. You never know, someone's day may be brightened because of it.

Think About It

"Real joy has little to do with what's in your head, rather what's in your heart and soul."
-Donald Hilliard

"Now and then it's good to pause in our pursuit of happiness and just be happy."
-Anonymous

"Happiness is perfume; you can't pour it on somebody else without getting a few drops on yourself."
-James Van Der Zee

INSPIRED LIVING

Friends and Friendships

26

There is no friendship sweeter than the one between you and Jesus Christ. He should be your best friend. If He is not, you should make Him your best friend now, because He said,

Scripture Says
"Greater love hath no man than this, that a man lay down his life for his friends."
--John 15:13

"I will never leave thee, nor forsake thee" (Hebrews 13:5b).

The first rule to making friends is to be friendly and to be a friend yourself. If other girls don't see you as nice and if they don't like your spirit, they will not want to be your friend. On the other hand, if you are friendly and kind, and not stuck-up, everyone will love being around you and will want to be friends with you.

My father has shared with me that you do not have to go searching for friends. God will give you true friends. When He does, it is something real special. True friends will tell you the truth about anything and everything. They will love you enough to tell you the truth even about yourself. If you and your friends are getting ready to go to a prom, and you have cookie crumbs on your mouth, wouldn't you want them to tell you that you have cookie crumbs on your mouth, so you won't embarrass yourself?

Make your time together with your friends meaningful and memorable. Girls sometimes tend to be catty and mean and get jealous of each other, but don't let that be the case with you. Don't encourage or participate in petty arguments, gossip, and lies. Encourage peace and love. It takes a lot of work to keep your relationships together. Just as you have to oil the hinges of a door when it gets rusty, you have to oil the hinges of your friendships with peace, kindness, inspiration, encouragement, help, honesty, and love. Tell your friends often how much you appreciate and enjoy their friendship.

Don't make friends with negative people because they will not encourage you or help you in life. All you can do for them is pray and let God change their hearts. You cannot change the people around you, but you can certainly change the people you are around.

True friends are great to have and you can have a lot of fun times together. You and your friends can:

- ♥ Go to the movies and to the mall together
- ♥ Study together
- ♥ Encourage each other
- ♥ Have an in-home Bible study
- ♥ Celebrate each other's birthday
- ♥ Cook dinner for all of your families
- ♥ Take each others' siblings to the park
- ♥ Go to the beauty salon or the spa
- ♥ Paint each other's nails

♥ Take lots of pictures together

There are a lot more things that you and your friends can do together. Make memories so that you can remember each other. But, most of all, make sure that Jesus Christ is your best friend.

Plan a sleepover for all your friends. Before you go to bed, quiet everyone, and tell them how much you appreciate their love and friendship.

Think About It

"A friend is someone who walks by your side."
-African Proverb

"A friend is someone who knows all your faults but still loves you."
-Unknown

" The supreme happiness of life is the conviction that one is loved; loved for oneself, or better yet, loved despite oneself."
-Victor Hugo

Inside Beauty

27

Girl, you are beautiful! You are made in the image of God, so stop wishing you could be like someone else. God gave you the features He wanted you to have. Stop wishing and just pray this prayer: "Lord, grant me the courage to change those things I can change about me, and grant me the grace to accept those things I cannot change." In other words, give me courage to change those things I can change such as my bad attitude, my disobedience, my dishonesty, my unkindness, etc., and give me the grace to accept my physical features as they are.

> **Scripture Says**
>
> "And Adam said, This is now bone of my bones, and flesh of my flesh: she shall be called Woman, because she was taken out of Man."
> --Genesis 2:23

Just as the world has their standard of beauty, in regards to who's in and who's out, who's pretty and who's not so pretty, God has His standards as well. His standards are not set on the outside, but they are contained on the inside—in the heart. Be pure in your heart and let the fruit of the Spirit radiate from your life to the lives of others. I pray every day for God to help me manifest the fruits of the Spirit in my life.

Real beauty does come from the heart and it shines through

in your life through your words and actions. *"And be renewed in the spirit of your mind; and that ye put on the new man, which after God is created in righteousness and true holiness"* (Ephesians 4:23-24). And this inner beauty is what is so attractive to many people. Whenever you start thinking and wishing you could look like someone else, just remember that outer beauty grows old and wrinkled. Inner beauty, however, grows more beautiful with age.

Be happy with the way God made you and begin to show your appreciation by doing the following:

♥ Take daily showers. They help keep body odors under control and they always make you feel better.

♥ Make sure your clothes are neat and clean. Don't go out with wrinkled clothes. Don't look like a hag. Take special care as to how you look everyday. And, never wear the same clothes twice in a week. A new day means a new look too.

♥ Take care of your hair. Wash it often. It's okay to perm it and get it styled, if your parents allow it. However, let me encourage you to wear your hair as natural as possible while you are young, so that it can grow healthy and strong. Also, don't cut your hair that much. A lot of young women cut their hair and then later on in life, they want it back and it won't grow back as they would like for it to. The Bible says that a woman's hair is her glory. So, love your hair and let it grow.

♥ Let someone you trust give you a good manicure and pedicure every two weeks or so. It's important to keep your hands, nails, and feet clean, because they can gather a lot of germs quickly. Keep your nails free of dirt so that you will always look clean and neat, even down to the small details.

♥ Look in the mirror before you step out the door. Make sure your face is clean and your appearance is presentable. You don't want people to talk about you behind your back because you missed something.

Love yourself the way God made you and show Him your appreciation for how He made you by taking care of your physical body and enhancing your inner beauty.

Celebrate

Save some money and go to a spa or a beauty salon. While you're there being pampered, release all the negative thoughts that you have about yourself. Begin to thank God for making you beautiful.

Think About It

"A woman's beauty lasts only as long as her disposition is sweet."

"Beauty is not in the face; beauty is a light in the heart."
-Kahlil Gibran

"People who possess a true inner beauty, their eyes are a little brighter, their skin a little more dewy. They vibrate at a different frequency."
-Cameron Diaz

Ladies Always Lead

28

There are some women in this world, who carry themselves with class and grace, thus earning the title "lady." Such women as Rosa Parks, Laura Bush, Condoleezza Rice, Dorothy Height, Eleanor Roosevelt, and many others, have a certain walk and look about them that make them stand out.

Scripture Says
"...And if I perish, I perish."
--Esther 4:16

Nancy Reagan once said: "I believe a woman gets more if she acts feminine." That's true. Perhaps you know some young women who don't carry themselves as ladies should. Do they get treated the same way as those who do? I do not think so.

Here are some things that some women do to get treated with respect--like a lady:

♥ Ladies do not stare at men. They just don't do it because it makes them look loose and easy. They mind their own business and do their own thing.

♥ Ladies do not act silly. They know that silly women do not get anywhere in life. They keep their minds on positive things and find good and constructive things to do with their time.

♥ Ladies do not lie. They know that if they tell a lie, people will not be able to trust them. They always speak the truth.

♥ Ladies live a "purpose-driven life". They know that they are here for a short time and that they must use that time doing something for God and for other people.

♥ Ladies do not live in clutter, chaos, and confusion. They keep their papers, books and personal belongings in order. They pay their bills on time. They are on time to meetings, etc. They are always ready to go anywhere and do anything because they have all their things in order.

♥ Ladies keep themselves pure. They are pure in their minds, bodies, hearts, and spirits. They know that purity shines through.

♥ Ladies do not tell all their business. If they are going through a tough time, they keep it to themselves and only tell close family and friends. When they have to go and do something or be around people, they leave their problems at home.

♥ Ladies sit, walk, and talk with class. They do not act like men—all rough and wild. They sit in a "lady-like" manner. They walk erect. They do not slouch, spread their legs, or curse. Everything that comes out of their mouth is kind and wise.

♥ Ladies are real. They do not live double lives–one way in front of one group of people and another way in front of another group of people. They are transparent, and because of that people love to be around them.

♥ Ladies think for themselves. They know that most of the world is made up of followers, so therefore, they think for themselves and lead other people to do right. They do not follow the crowd, the crowd follows them.

Well, these are just some things that women do so that they can be treated with respect. Remember, ladies carry themselves with class and dignity. They do it so no one can say anything negative about them. That is one of the best feelings in the world. Ladies always lead!

Look back over the past week and evaluate yourself as to whether or not you carried yourself like a lady. Purpose to live like a Godly lady everyday.

Think About It

"If the first woman God ever made was strong enough to turn the world upside down all alone... women together ought to be able to turn it back, and get it right side up again."
-Sojourner Truth

"A good leader not only knows where he is going, but he can persuade other people to go along with him."

"You may not have started out life in the best of circumstances. But if you can find a mission in life worth working for and believe in yourself, nothing can stop you from achieving success."
-Kemmons Wilson

Live a Great Life and Enjoy It!

*S*hakespeare said: "All the world's a stage and the men and women are merely players. They have their entrances and their exits." He was so right. You aren't going to be here forever. So, it is best to do what you can in all the ways you can, live a great life, and enjoy your life, while you have your turn on the stage of life because one day you will have to "exit".

> **Scripture Says**
> "Delight thyself also in the LORD: and he shall give thee the desires of thine heart."
> --Psalm 37:4

I have met some young people in my short life, who do not enjoy their lives. To make matters worse, it seems they have no clue as to how to begin to enjoy it. I believe that if we would take time out of our busy schedules, and begin to really pay attention to the small things in life, then we can truly learn what it means to enjoy our lives.

Jesus Christ said in John 10:10b: *"I am come that they might have life, and that they might have it more abundantly."* Jesus Christ wants you to enjoy every minute of your life, even the difficult times.

One of the things my papa has taught me is that even when you are going through trouble or through a difficult time in

155

life is to actually enjoy the trouble as well. It is part of life. If I find something hard, I put it in the hands of the Lord, because nothing is too hard for Him to handle. If I feel like something is not going quite the way that I would like for it to go, I have learned to put the whole situation in the Lord's hands, because however it turns out, I know it will be for my good.

Don't search for a perfect life because nobody has a perfect life or will have a perfect life while on this earth. People with a lot of money, cars, and houses don't even have perfect lives. Some of these people can't enjoy the life they have because they are too worried about getting more. With that said, here are some ways to enjoy your life:

♥ Make every day a good day. Don't let people, problems, or your emotions cause you to have a bad day. Whatever is on your agenda to do for a certain day, do it and enjoy doing it. Remember, nobody or nothing can mess up your day unless you let them.

♥ Love every moment. A lot of people tend to build up to big events, get excited, and maybe even enjoy the event; but after the big event has come and gone, they fall into a depression. Why? Because they live in and for the happenings. You will never be happy and be able to enjoy anything if you are dependent upon the "happenings". What is happening is Jesus Christ. He is the only One you can get excited about and stay excited about. He is always happening. Learn to enjoy getting up out of bed, getting dressed, going to school, going to work, doing your chores, etc. Learn to enjoy the little things like putting in your earrings or tying your sneakers.

♥ Don't hang around negative people. Nothing excites negative people more than other negative people. All they enjoy is gossip and foolishness. As a girl who God wants, you will not be able to enjoy your life if you are always hanging around negative people.

♥ Give to others. You don't always have to give material things. You can give a smile or a hug. Life is not all about you or me, it is about the Lord and other people. When we enjoy making other people's day brighter, we can enjoy our day more.

♥ Don't worry. Don't fret. Whatever happens in your life, God has a reason for it. He saw everything that has happened in your life and that will happen in your life before He created you. So, He will protect you.

God wants you to have life abundantly and He wants you to enjoy it. Don't worry about where you have been. Don't worry about where you are going. Enjoy the present. Enjoy today. Enjoy the moment. Enjoy your life. Let God fill you with His *"peace that passeth all understanding"* and His *"joy unspeakable."* Don't wait for a certain time to enjoy your life. Enjoy the life God gave you today!

 Determine in your heart to make everyday a good day and to enjoy it to its fullest. Say out loud, "It's gonna be a good day."

Think About It

"You don't get to choose how you're going to die. Or when. You can only decide how you're going to live. Now."
-Joan Baez

"It's faith in something and enthusiasm for something that makes a life worth living."
-Oliver Wendell Holmes

"What I do today is important because I am exchanging a day of my life for it."
-Hugh Mulligan

Conclusion: On Living "the Girl God wants" Lifestyle

$\mathcal{I}$ have had a wonderful time, talking with you and sharing with you some of the things that are helping me each day to be "the Girl God wants". Now, before I go, I want to leave

> ### Scripture Says
> "I have fought a good fight, I have finished my course, I have kept the faith: Henceforth there is laid up for me a crown of righteousness..."
> —2 Timothy 4:7-8

you with twelve things to take with you each day on your journey in God's plan and purpose for your life. These twelve things make up what I call "the Girl God wants" lifestyle. If you apply these twelve basic things to your life, I guarantee you that God will give you a blessed, happy, productive, and great life that you will enjoy. Here we go:

♥ Pray at least each morning and each night, no matter what.

♥ Read at least one chapter in the Bible each morning and each night, no matter what.

♥ Put your faith in God and know that you *"can do all things through Christ which strengtheneth you"*.

161

♥ Be obedient to God from your heart.

♥ Study hard and get a great education.

♥ Ask God for wisdom and understanding.

♥ Follow your dreams and do not let anyone stop you from reaching your goals. Be "purpose-driven" and live with your goals and plans in mind.

♥ Love your family, and help them in any way that you can.

♥ Obey your parents in all things.

♥ When you get on top in life, be sure to reach behind you and help another sister up.

♥ Keep yourself pure in body, mind, soul, and spirit.

♥ Live your life to its fullest extent and enjoy it!

Sisters, I love you all, and I want you to know that God loves you and He wants you to be all that you can be for His glory. I look forward to talking with you next time in *The Girl God Wants Devotional and Journal*.

Celebrate

Now Girls, Let's Go Out There, Be "the Girl God wants", and Change the World for God, One Step at a Time!

Grace
Favor
and
Blessings!

Daniella

INSPIRATIONS

Books

1. *Were It Not for Grace: Stories from Women after God's Own Heart*, by Leslie Montgomery

2. *The Real Deal: A Spiritual Guide for Black Teen Girls*, by Billie Montgomery Cook

3. *Seven Secrets to Sexual Purity*, by Dannah Gresh

4. *And the Bride Wore White*, by Dannah Gresh

5. *On a Positive Note*, by CeCe Winans

6. *A Young Woman After God's Own Heart*, by Elizabeth George

7. *Let's Talk: Good Stuff for Girlfriends about God, Guys, and Growing Up*, by Danae Dobson

8. *A Young Woman's Walk with God*, by Elizabeth George

9. *The Payton Skyy Series*, by Stephanie Perry Moore

10. *The Virtuous Girl*, by Danita Whyte

11. *Letters to Young Black Women*, by Daniel Whyte III

12. *Battlefield of the Mind for Teens* by Joyce Meyer

13. *Prayer of Jabez for Teens*, by Bruce Wilkinson

14. *When Teens Pray*, by Cheri Fuller & Ron Luce

15. *Secret Keeper: The Delicate Power of Modesty*, by Dannah Gresh

16. *Every Teen Girl's Little Pink Book*, by Cathy Bartel

17. *Girls of Grace*, by Point of Grace

18. *Beauty Secrets: Tips for Teens from the Ultimate Makeover Artist*, by Deborah Newman & Rachel Newman

19. *Daughters of Heaven*, by Suzanne Rentz

20. *Radiant: Discovering Beauty from the Inside Out*, by Chandra Peele

21. *Always Sisters!*, by CeCe Winans

22. *Spiritual Lessons for My Sisters*, by Natasha Munson

23. *For Young Women Only*, by Shaunti Feldhahn & Lisa Rice

24. *Every Young Woman's Battle*, by Shannon Ethridge & Stephen Arterburn

25. *The Power of a Praying Teen*, by Stormie Omartian

26. *Simply Divine Series*, by Jacquelin Thomas

INSPIRATIONS

Music

1. *Purified*, by CeCe Winans

2. *Victory Live!*, by Tye Tribbett & GA

3. *Alabaster Box*, by CeCe Winans

4. *Lifesong*, by Casting Crowns

5. *Real*, by Israel & New Breed

6. *Beauty has Grace*, by Jaci Velasquez

7. *Hero*, by Kirk Franklin

8. *The Nu Nation Project*, by Kirk Franklin

9. *I Owe You*, by Kierra "Kiki" Sheard

10. *Testimony*, by Virtue

11. *Redeemer*, by Nicole C. Mullen

12. *Genuine*, by Stacie Orrico

13. *I Need You Now*, Smokie Norful

14. *No Limits*, by Martha Munizzi

15. *Say the Name*, by Martha Munizzi

16. *Bringing It All Together*, by Vickie Winans

17. *This Moment*, by Steven Curtis Chapman

18. *It's So God*, by Brian Free and Assurance

19. *Free to Fly*, by Point of Grace

20. *He's Been Faithful*, by Vicki Yohe

21. *Higher Definition*, by The Cross Movement

22. *The J Moss Project V2*, by J Moss

23. *Thy Kingdom Come*, by CeCe Winans

24. *Stand Out*, by Tye Tribbett & GA

INSPIRATIONS
Magazines

1. Brio Magazine

2. Teen Virtue Magazine

3. Realiteen Magazine

4. Brio and Beyond Magazine

5. Ignite Your Faith Magazine

6. Teens in Motion Magazine

7. Campus Life Magazine

8. Guideposts Sweet 16 Magazine

9. Teen Voices Magazine

10. YouthWalk

11. Christian Music Magazine

INSPIRATIONS

 ## Websites

1. www.CeCeWinans.com

2. www.PureFreedom.org

3. www.TheVirtuousGirl.org

4. www.BrioMag.com

5. www.VickiCourtney.com

6. www.Shaunti.com

7. www.CeeCeeMichaela.com

8. www.StephaniePerryMoore.com

9. www.ElizabethGeorge.com

10. www.RealTeenFaith.com

11. www.IAmWorththeWait.com

12. www.ChristianityToday.com/teens

13. www.LetterstoYoungBlackWomen.org

Visit Me on MySpace at:

Myspace.com/theGirlGodWants

Made in the USA
Lexington, KY
30 April 2015